WOMEN'S EDITION

THE 16-BAR
POP/ROCK AUDITION
100 HIT SONGS EXCERPTED FOR SUCCESSFUL AUDITIONS

COMPILED AND EDITED BY MICHAEL DANSICKER

ISBN 978-1-4234-6886-8

7777 W. BLUEMOUND RD. P.O. BOX 13819 MILWAUKEE, WI 53213

For all works contained herein:
Unauthorized copying, arranging, adapting, recording, Internet posting, public performance,
or other distribution of the printed music in this publication is an infringement of copyright.
Infringers are liable under the law.

Visit Hal Leonard Online at
www.halleonard.com

CONTENTS

8 **Against All Odds**
PHIL COLLINS

10 **Ain't No Other Man**
CHRISTINA AGUILERA

12 **All by Myself**
CELINE DION

14 **All My Loving**
THE BEATLES

16 **All Through the Night**
CYNDI LAUPER

15 **Alone**
HEART

18 **Anyone Who Had a Heart**
DIONNE WARWICK

20 **Band of Gold**
FREDA PAYNE; KIMBERLY LOCKE

22 **Beautiful**
CHRISTINA AGUILERA

21 **Before Your Love**
KELLY CLARKSON

24 **Breakaway**
KELLY CLARKSON

26 **Breaking Free**
ZAC EFRON & VANESSA ANNE HUDGENS

28 **Breaking Up Is Hard to Do**
NEIL SEDAKA

30 **Can't Help Falling in Love**
ELVIS PRESLEY; UB40

32 **Crazy**
PATSY CLINE

34 **Crazy on You**
HEART

36 **Dancing in the Street**
MARTHA & THE VANDELLAS

38 **Dedicated to the One I Love**
THE SHIRELLES; THE MAMAS & THE PAPAS

40 **Don't Cry Out Loud**
MELISSA MANCHESTER

42 **Don't Stop**
FLEETWOOD MAC

35 **Eight Days a Week**
THE BEATLES

44 **Ever Ever After**
CARRIE UNDERWOOD

46 **Every Breath You Take**
THE POLICE

48 **Fire and Ice**
PAT BENATAR

50 **A Girl's Night Out**
THE JUDDS

52 **Girls Just Want to Have Fun**
CYNDI LAUPER

51 **Give Me All Night**
CARLY SIMON

54 **Heatwave**
MARTHA & THE VANDELLAS

56 **Here You Come Again**
DOLLY PARTON

58 **Hero**
MARIAH CAREY

60 **Hit Me with Your Best Shot**
PAT BENATAR

62 **Holding Out for a Hero**
BONNIE TYLER

64	**Hopelessly Devoted to You** OLIVIA NEWTON-JOHN	90	**It's All Wrong, But It's All Right** DOLLY PARTON
66	**How Am I Supposed to Live Without You** MICHAEL BOLTON	92	**It's So Easy** THE CRICKETS; LINDA RONSTADT
68	**I Can't Make You Love Me** BONNIE RAITT	94	**It's Too Late** CAROLE KING
70	**I Feel the Earth Move** CAROLE KING	96	**Let It Be** THE BEATLES
72	**I Need You** MARC ANTHONY	98	**Listen** BEYONCÉ
74	**I Say a Little Prayer** DIONNE WARWICK	100	**Love Will Keep Us Together** THE CAPTAIN & TENNILLE
65	**I Wanna Love You Forever** JESSICA SIMPSON	102	**Love You I Do** JENNIFER HUDSON
76	**I Will** THE BEATLES	101	**A Moment Like This** KELLY CLARKSON
77	**I Will Always Love You** DOLLY PARTON; WHITNEY HOUSTON	104	**More Today Than Yesterday** SPIRAL STAIRCASE
78	**I Will Remember You** SARAH McLACHLAN	106	**My Father** JUDY COLLINS
80	**I'll Be There** THE JACKSON 5; MARIAH CAREY	105	**My Guy** MARY WELLS
82	**I'll Stand by You** PRETENDERS; CARRIE UNDERWOOD	108	**(You Make Me Feel Like) A Natural Woman** ARETHA FRANKLIN; CELINE DION; KELLY CLARKSON
81	**I'm a Believer** THE MONKEES; SMASH MOUTH	110	**One Fine Day** THE CHIFFONS
84	**If I Can't Have You** YVONNE ELLIMAN; BEE GEES	112	**Piece of My Heart** JANIS JOPLIN
86	**If I Fell** THE BEATLES	114	**The Power of Love** CELINE DION
88	**Imagine** JOHN LENNON	116	**Reflection** CHRISTINA AGUILERA
87	**In My Life** THE BEATLES	118	**Remember Me This Way** JORDAN HILL

Page	Title	Artist
111	**River Deep - Mountain High**	CELINE DION
120	**Save the Best for Last**	VANESSA WILLIAMS
122	**Saving All My Love for You**	WHITNEY HOUSTON
124	**So Far Away**	CAROLE KING
126	**Solitaire**	ELVIS PRESLEY; THE CARPENTERS; CLAY AIKEN
128	**Somebody to Love**	JEFFERSON AIRPLANE
130	**Something to Talk About**	BONNIE RAITT
132	**Sometimes When We Touch**	DAN HILL
134	**Superstar**	THE CARPENTERS
136	**Sweet Dreams (Are Made of This)**	EURYTHMICS
138	**These Dreams**	HEART
140	**Thing Called Love**	BONNIE RAITT
142	**This Ain't a Love Song**	BON JOVI
144	**Time After Time**	CYNDI LAUPER
146	**True Colors**	CYNDI LAUPER; PHIL COLLINS
148	**Unfaithful**	RIHANNA
150	**Walk on By**	DIONNE WARWICK
152	**Want Ads**	THE HONEY CONE
154	**We've Only Just Begun**	THE CARPENTERS
156	**What About Love?**	HEART
158	**What Am I to You**	NORAH JONES
160	**When There Was Me and You**	VANESSA ANNE HUDGENS
133	**When Will I Be Loved**	LINDA RONSTADT
164	**Where Do Broken Hearts Go**	WHITNEY HOUSTON
166	**Where the Boys Are**	CONNIE FRANCIS
168	**Why Do Fools Fall in Love**	FRANKIE LYMON & THE TEENAGERS
162	**Will You Still Love Me Tomorrow**	THE SHIRELLES
163	**Without You**	BADFINGER; MARIAH CAREY
170	**Wouldn't It Be Nice**	THE BEACH BOYS
172	**You Can't Hurry Love**	THE SUPREMES; PHIL COLLINS
174	**You Keep Me Hangin' On**	THE SHIRELLES
176	**You Learn**	ALANIS MORISSETTE
178	**You Raise Me Up**	JOSH GROBAN
180	**You'll Be in My Heart**	PHIL COLLINS

PREFACE

The standard "open singer's call" has become the most readily available opportunity for aspiring musical theatre actors eager to introduce their talent to the professional creative teams of Broadway and touring productions. In order to accommodate the large numbers of talented, young performers, New York casting professionals have established the 16-bar excerpt as the industry standard.

THE 16-BAR AUDITION

The selection should be no longer than thirty seconds and should clearly represent the style and spirit of the musical being cast. If the song is written in a very fast cut time, 32 bars would be appropriate. Dialects should be avoided; and unless specifically noted, the lyric should be sung in English. Your goal is to select the *best* 16 bars of the song chosen. Selecting an arbitrary 16 bars is not always useful. Because standard theatre music (written before 1970) often adheres to the 32-bar song form (AABA), it is fairly easy to excerpt and edit for audition purposes. Contemporary musical theatre writing faithfully serves the drama its writers are musicalizing but is rarely successfully consolidated for 16-bar cuttings. Keep the introduction short (a bell tone is fine) and clearly mark your music! Any transposition should be neatly written out, and original material from camp shows, revues, and your best friend's newest musical should be left at home. Indicate the tempo clearly to the accompanist.

THE CHANGING SOUND OF BROADWAY

While few songs written for new Broadway musicals have hit the record charts as viable best sellers, there has been a new addition to today's musical theatre genre. That is: The Jukebox Musical. Ticket buyers, shelling out a great deal of money for their entertainment, are often excited about hearing the old, familiar songs of beloved Pop artists showcased in a legitimate theatre vehicle. ABBA, Elvis, Green Day, The Beach Boys, Dolly Parton, Buddy Holly, Bob Dylan, John Lennon, Frankie Valli, Billy Joel, Johnny Cash and Queen have all been represented in London's West End and on the Great White Way. In addition, shows based on Disney animated classics (i.e. *The Lion King*, *The Little Mermaid*, and *Mary Poppins*) and TV productions (i.e. *High School Musical 1, 2,* and *3* and *Glee*) have become part of the new tradition. The songs from Broadway properties reinvented for film (i.e. *Dreamgirls*, *Rent*, *Hairspray* and *Nine*) are now an important addition to today's audition repertory. TV's *American Idol* has introduced a new generation to the Pop music of past decades as well as the Broadway classics of yesteryear. All are approached in a contemporary, stylized way, and their impact on young performers can not be discounted. No longer can the complete musical theatre performer ignore the Pop/Rock music of the last fifty years. It is now a living part of the Broadway Songbook. The audition landscape has changed, but good singing technique and vocal discipline are invaluable in successfully utilizing this material for auditions.

THE CHALLENGE

Music created and recorded by popular artists has the advantage of being produced in a recording studio. Background vocals and intricate programmed drums/sequenced synth tracks are as much a part of the fabric of the song as the actual music and lyric. Obviously, the accompaniment of a theatre audition pianist will never evoke the punch and fill of a produced musical orchestration. However, stripping the song down to basic elements can be an advantage. While the dramatic element of a true theatre song is ultimately more specific in intention and ultimate performance, many Pop songs have a winning simplicity and strong emotional line. It is up to the performer to choose how far the dramatic context of the song can be developed and to decide how far the vocal envelope can be exploited at an audition. But total commitment to your work as actor and singer is imperative. Don't forget to impart the joy of being a musical theatre actor.

VOCAL RANGES

You can't show everything in 16 bars! Your audition is an introduction of your vocal and acting expertise to a production team. I have never approved of interpolated high notes in 16-bar selections. A note inserted to show range, with no cohesive relation to the phrase, will not work favorably for you. However, the transposition of a selection to a place in your voice that is exciting and attractive is standard procedure. Remember, the upper limits of range are "the norm" in today's commercial market. It is not unusual to expect ladies to belt an E5. Baritones are requested to sing G5, and many tenors are required to have a high C6. It is a world of "higher and louder!" And legit sopranos must have the courage to tackle material outside of the standard musical theatre rep.

SELECTIONS IN THESE VOLUMES

I have attempted to include a wide variety of composition and style in these volumes. It should never be the intention of any actor to mimic a particular artist. Work with the lyric and the musical setting to create your own take on the material. I know you will find that these songs are worth investigating in a dramatic context. Don't be afraid to use a song that is used often at auditions. The creative team is looking for your "take" on the material. Every actor is unique, and your understanding of a song that is commonly sung just might be that special something that gets you a callback.

LESS THAN 16 BARS

Many casting directors in New York/L.A. auditions have scaled back the 16-bar standard cutting to 8 bars in order to accommodate the large number of singers attending various calls. Of course, limiting a performance to 8 bars tends to strip the dramatic integrity from the audition! However, an experienced creative team will certainly note your accuracy of pitch and placement. Your negotiating a song's range and phrasing challenges can also be determined in a shortened audition cutting.

BE PREPARED!

It is very important that if a 16-bar selection becomes a part of your audition book that you also take the time to learn and master the entire piece. There is always the chance a director will say: "That was sensational! Let's hear the whole song!"

Michael Dansicker
New York City
May, 2010

MICHAEL DANSICKER has worked as arranger, composer, musical director and pianist on over 100 Broadway and Off-Broadway productions. He wrote the dance and incidental music for Rachel Portman's *Little House on the Prairie* (starring Melissa Gilbert) and the songs for Jim Davis's *Garfield Live* (with Bill Meade). Last season, he arranged, scored, and supervised Bob Dylan and Twyla Tharp's *The Times They Are a Changin'*. His new musical *Shooting Star: The Bobby Driscoll Story* (directed by Francesca Zambello) is currently in development. He served as vocal consultant to the hit films: *Elf* (New Line Cinema), *Analyze That* (WB), *Meet the Parents* (Universal) and scored the dances for Paramount's *Brain Donors*. In the world of Concert Dance: ABT, Twyla Tharp, Agnes de Mille, JOFFREY, Jerome Robbins, Donald McKayle, Geoffrey Holder, Mikhail Baryshnikov and Kenny Ortega. He has worked as creative consultant to Walt Disney Entertainment and is one of the country's leading vocal specialists and session pianists.

Special thanks to Rick Walters at Hal Leonard, Fran Charnas (Boston Conservatory), Scot Reese and Carmen Balthrop (University of Maryland), Clay James (Montclair State University), Michael Cassara, and the "Dean" of Broadway Casting – JAY BINDER!

AGAINST ALL ODDS
(Take a Look at Me Now)
from *Against All Odds*
recorded by Phil Collins
excerpt

Words and Music by
PHIL COLLINS

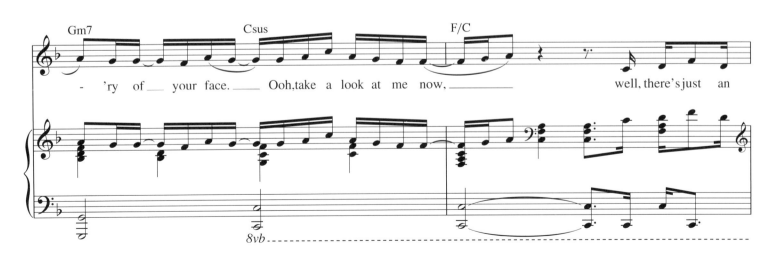

© 1984 EMI Golden Torch Music Corp. and Philip Collins Ltd.
All Rights except Synchronization Rights Jointly Administered by EMI Golden Torch Music Corp. and EMI April Music Inc. on behalf of Philip Collins Ltd.
Synchronization Rights Exclusively Administered by EMI Golden Torch Music Corp.
All Rights Reserved   International Copyright Secured   Used by Permission

AIN'T NO OTHER MAN
recorded by Christina Aguilera

excerpt

Words and Music by CHRISTINA AGUILERA,
KARA DioGUARDI, CHRIS MARTIN,
CHARLES ROANE and HAROLD BEATTY

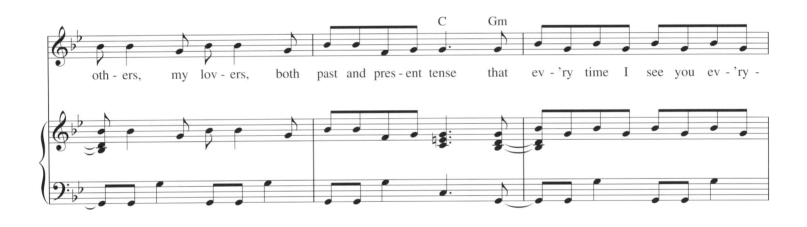

Copyright © 2006 by Universal Music - Careers, Xtina Music, Bug Music Inc., Gifted Pearl Music, Works Of Mart, Inc., Tricia Sounds Music and Iza Music Corp.
All Rights for Xtina Music Administered by Universal Music - Careers
All Rights for Iza Music Corp. Administered by The Clyde Otis Music Group, Inc.
International Copyright Secured   All Rights Reserved

ALL BY MYSELF
recorded by Celine Dion
excerpt

Music by SERGEI RACHMANINOFF
Words and Additional Music by ERIC CARMEN

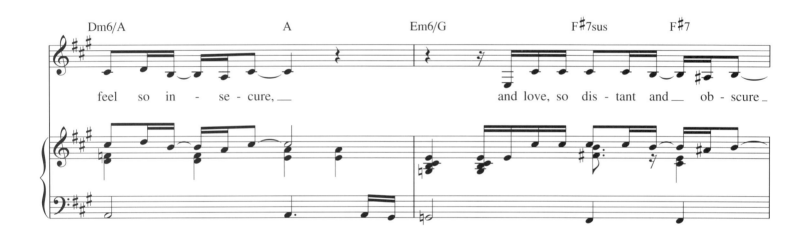

Copyright © 1975 ERIC CARMEN MUSIC, INC.
Copyright Renewed
All Rights Controlled and Administered by UNIVERSAL - SONGS OF POLYGRAM INTERNATIONAL, INC.
All Rights Reserved   Used by Permission

ALL MY LOVING

recorded by The Beatles

excerpt

Words and Music by JOHN LENNON and PAUL McCARTNEY

Copyright © 1963, 1964 Sony/ATV Music Publishing LLC
Copyright Renewed
All Rights Administered by Sony/ATV Music Publishing LLC, 8 Music Square West, Nashville, TN 37203
International Copyright Secured All Rights Reserved

ALL THROUGH THE NIGHT

recorded by Cyndi Lauper

excerpt

Words and Music by
JULES SHEAR

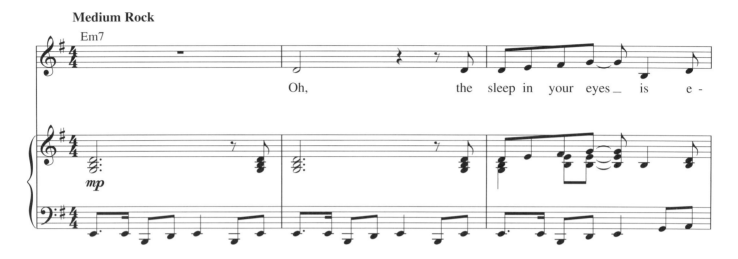

Copyright © 1982 SONGS OF UNIVERSAL, INC., Funzalo Music LTD. and Juters Music
All Rights Controlled and Administered by SONGS OF UNIVERSAL, INC.
All Rights Reserved   Used by Permission

BREAKAWAY
from *The Princess Diaries 2: Royal Engagement*
recorded by Kelly Clarkson

excerpt

Words and Music by BRIDGET BENENATE,
AVRIL LAVIGNE and MATTHEW GERRARD

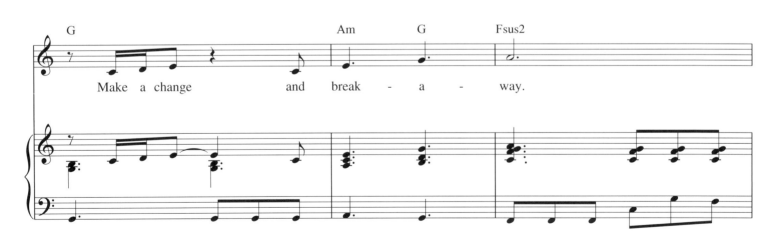

Copyright © 2004 Bug Music-Music Of Windswept, Friends Of Seagulls Music Publishing, Blotter Music,
Almo Music Corp., Avril Lavigne Publishing Ltd., WB Music Corp. and G Matt Music
All Rights for Friends Of Seagulls Music Publishing and Blotter Music Administered by Bug Music-Music Of Windswept
All Rights for Avril Lavigne Publishing Ltd. Controlled and Administered by Almo Music Corp.
All Rights Reserved   Used by Permission

BREAKING FREE
from the Disney Channel Original Movie *High School Musical*
recorded by Zac Efron & Vanessa Anne Hudgens

excerpt

Words and Music by
JAMIE HOUSTON

© 2005 Walt Disney Music Company
All Rights Reserved Used by Permission

BREAKING UP IS HARD TO DO

recorded by Neil Sedaka

excerpt

Words and Music by HOWARD GREENFIELD
and NEIL SEDAKA

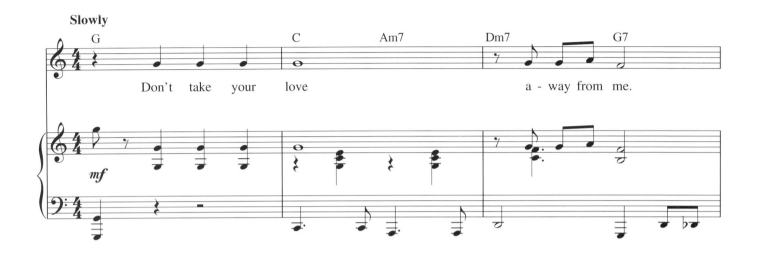

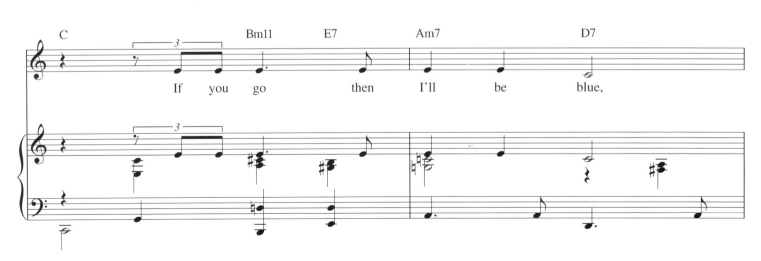

© 1962 (Renewed 1990) SCREEN GEMS-EMI MUSIC INC. and UNIVERSAL MUSIC - CAREERS
All Rights Reserved   International Copyright Secured   Used by Permission

CAN'T HELP FALLING IN LOVE

recorded by Elvis Presley; UB40

excerpt

Words and Music by GEORGE DAVID WEISS,
HUGO PERETTI and LUIGI CREATORE

Copyright © 1961; Renewed 1989 Gladys Music (ASCAP)
Worldwide Rights for Gladys Music Administered by Cherry Lane Music Publishing Company, Inc.
International Copyright Secured   All Rights Reserved

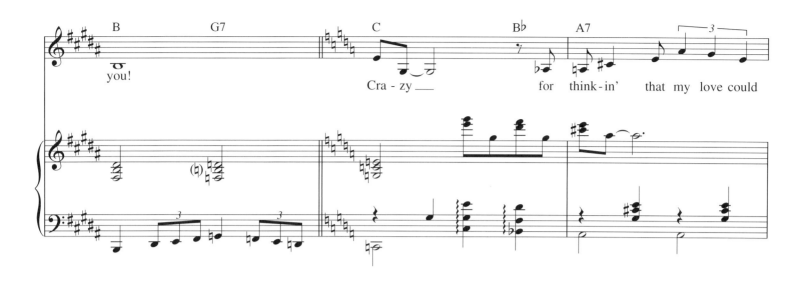
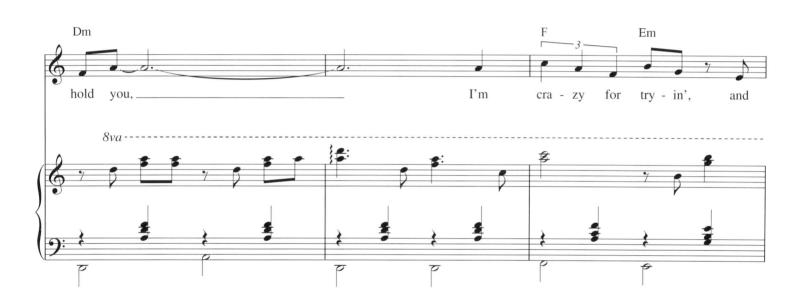

EIGHT DAYS A WEEK

recorded by The Beatles

excerpt

Words and Music by JOHN LENNON
and PAUL McCARTNEY

Copyright © 1964 Sony/ATV Music Publishing LLC
Copyright Renewed
All Rights Administered by Sony/ATV Music Publishing LLC, 8 Music Square West, Nashville, TN 37203
International Copyright Secured   All Rights Reserved

DANCING IN THE STREET
recorded by Martha & The Vandellas

excerpt

Words and Music by MARVIN GAYE,
IVY HUNTER and WILLIAM STEVENSON

© 1964 (Renewed 1992) FCG MUSIC, NMG MUSIC, MGIII MUSIC, JOBETE MUSIC CO., INC. and STONE AGATE MUSIC
All Rights Controlled and Administered by EMI APRIL MUSIC INC. and EMI BLACKWOOD MUSIC INC. on behalf of
JOBETE MUSIC CO., INC. and STONE AGATE MUSIC (A Division of JOBETE MUSIC CO., INC.)
All Rights Reserved   International Copyright Secured   Used by Permission

DEDICATED TO THE ONE I LOVE
recorded by The Shirelles; The Mamas & The Papas

excerpt

Words and Music by LOWMAN PAULING
and RALPH BASS

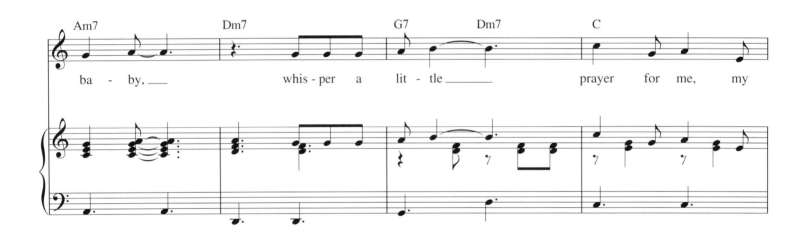

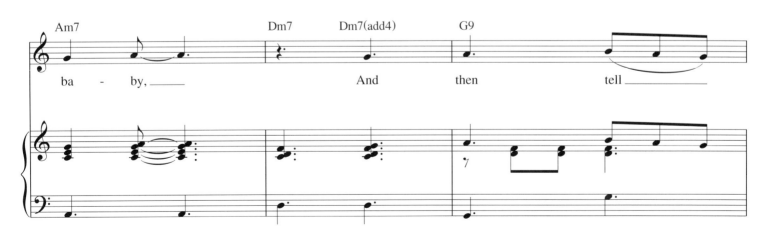

Copyright © 1957, 1967, 1971 SONGS OF UNIVERSAL, INC.
Copyright Renewed, Assigned to LOWMAN PAULING and SONGS OF UNIVERSAL, INC.
All Rights in the United States for the interest of LOWMAN PAULING Controlled by FORT KNOX MUSIC INC. and BUG MUSIC-TRIO MUSIC COMPANY
All Rights Reserved   Used by Permission

DON'T CRY OUT LOUD
(We Don't Cry Out Loud)
recorded by Melissa Manchester

excerpt

Words and Music by PETER ALLEN
and CAROLE BAYER SAGER

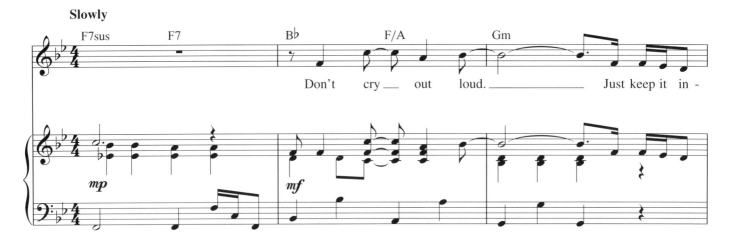
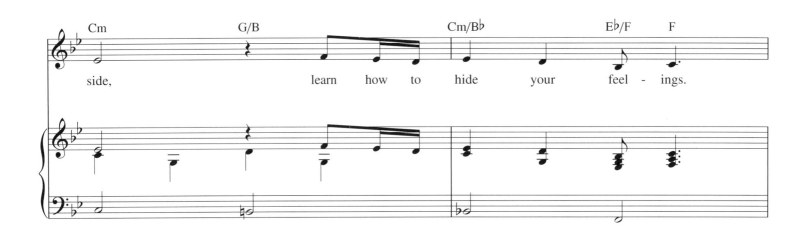

Copyright © 1976 IRVING MUSIC, INC., WOOLNOUGH MUSIC, INC. and BEGONIA MELODIES, INC.
Copyright Renewed
All Rights for WOOLNOUGH MUSIC, INC. Controlled and Administered by IRVING MUSIC, INC.
All Rights for BEGONIA MELODIES, INC. Controlled and Administered by SONGS OF UNIVERSAL, INC.
All Rights Reserved   Used by Permission

DON'T STOP
recorded by Fleetwood Mac
excerpt

Words and Music by
CHRISTINE McVIE

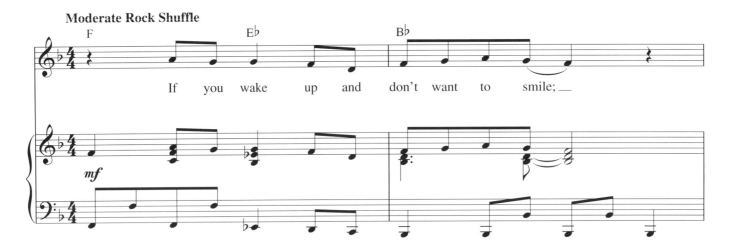

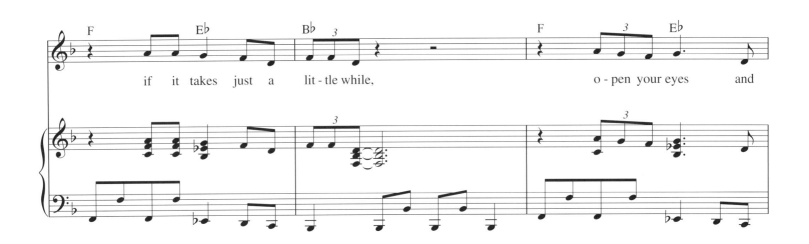

Copyright © 1976 by Universal Music - Careers
Copyright Renewed
International Copyright Secured   All Rights Reserved

EVER EVER AFTER

from Walt Disney Pictures' *Enchanted*

recorded by Carrie Underwood

excerpt

Music by ALAN MENKEN
Lyrics by STEPHEN SCHWARTZ

© 2007 Wonderland Music Company, Inc. and Walt Disney Music Company
All Rights Reserved Used by Permission

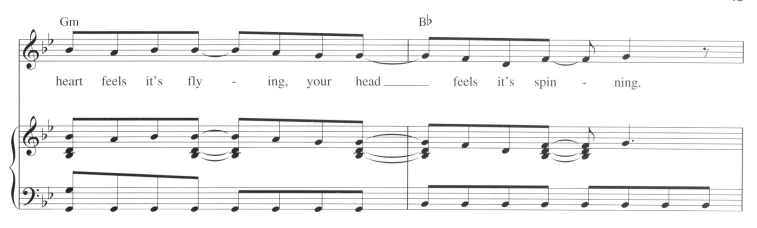
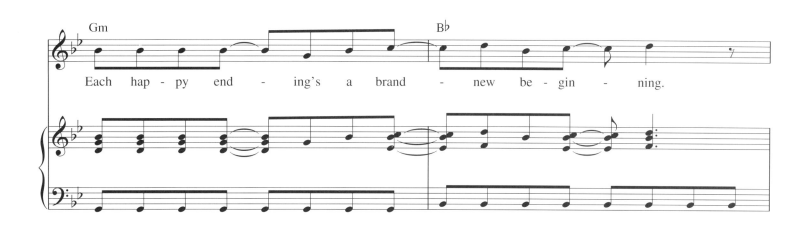
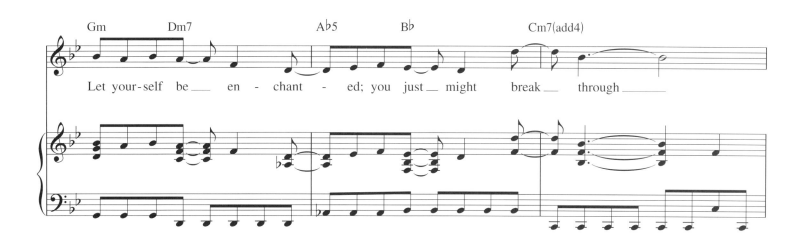

EVERY BREATH YOU TAKE

recorded by The Police

excerpt

Music and Lyrics by
STING

© 1983 G.M. SUMNER
Administered by EMI MUSIC PUBLISHING LIMITED
All Rights Reserved   International Copyright Secured   Used by Permission

FIRE AND ICE
recorded by Pat Benatar
excerpt

Words and Music by TOM KELLY,
SCOTT SHEETS and PAT BENATAR

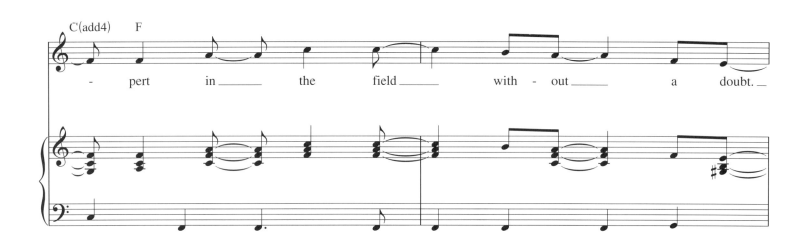

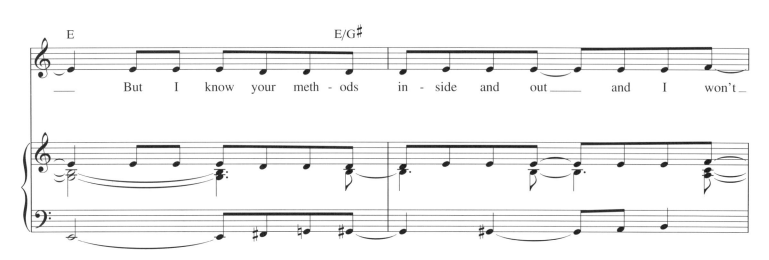

Copyright © 1981 Sony/ATV Music Publishing LLC, Chrysalis Music, Big Tooth Music and Discott Music
All Rights on behalf of Sony/ATV Music Publishing LLC Administered by Sony/ATV Music Publishing LLC, 8 Music Square West, Nashville, TN 37203
All Rights on behalf of Big Tooth Music and Discott Music Administered by Chrysalis Music
International Copyright Secured   All Rights Reserved

GIRLS JUST WANT TO HAVE FUN

recorded by Cyndi Lauper

excerpt

Words and Music by
ROBERT HAZARD

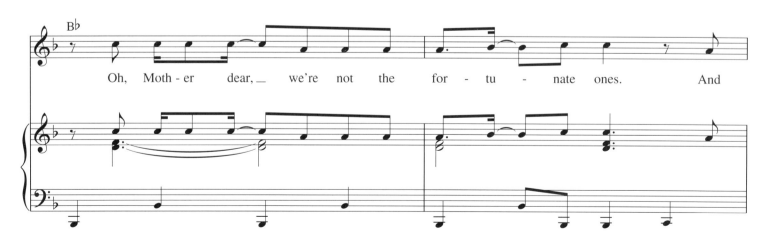

Copyright © 1979 Sony/ATV Music Publishing LLC
All Rights Administered by Sony/ATV Music Publishing LLC, 8 Music Square West, Nashville, TN 37203
International Copyright Secured   All Rights Reserved

HEATWAVE
(Love Is Like a Heatwave)
recorded by Martha & The Vandellas
excerpt

Words and Music by EDWARD HOLLAND, LAMONT DOZIER and BRIAN HOLLAND

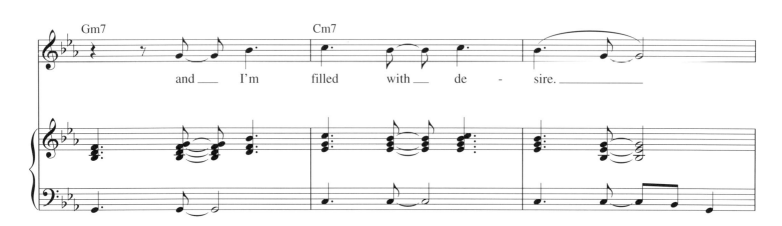

© 1963 (Renewed 1991) JOBETE MUSIC CO., INC.
All Rights Controlled and Administered by EMI BLACKWOOD MUSIC INC. on behalf of STONE AGATE MUSIC (A Division of JOBETE MUSIC CO., INC.)
All Rights Reserved   International Copyright Secured   Used by Permission

HERE YOU COME AGAIN

recorded by Dolly Parton

excerpt

Words by CYNTHIA WEIL
Music by BARRY MANN

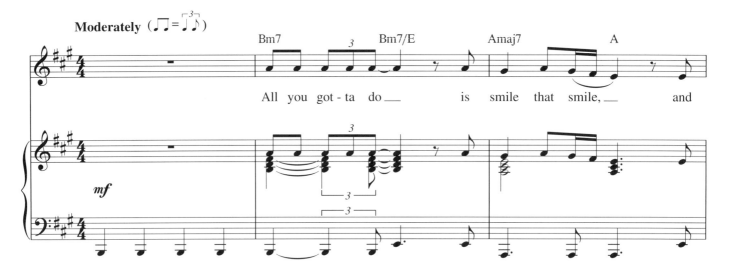

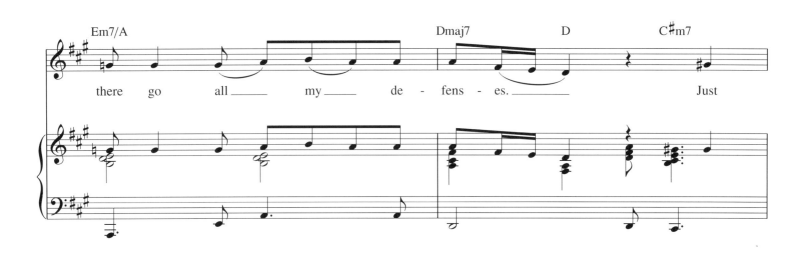

© 1977 (Renewed 2005) SCREEN GEMS-EMI MUSIC INC. and SUMMERHILL SONGS INC.
All Rights Controlled and Administered by SCREEN GEMS-EMI MUSIC INC.
All Rights Reserved   International Copyright Secured   Used by Permission

HERO
recorded by Mariah Carey
excerpt

Words and Music by MARIAH CAREY
and WALTER AFANASIEFF

Copyright © 1993 RYE SONGS, WB MUSIC CORP. and WALLYWORLD MUSIC
All Rights for RYE SONGS Controlled and Administered by SONGS OF UNIVERSAL, INC.
All Rights for WALLYWORLD MUSIC Controlled and Administered by WB MUSIC CORP.
All Rights Reserved   Used by Permission

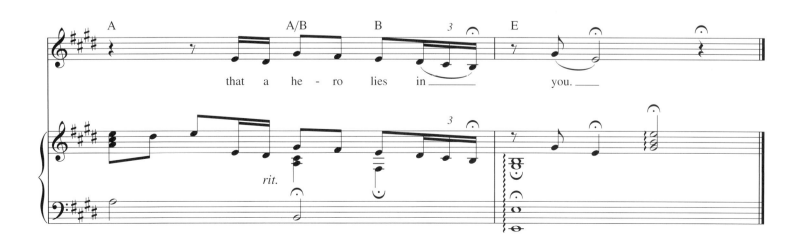

HIT ME WITH YOUR BEST SHOT

recorded by Pat Benatar

excerpt

Words and Music by
EDDIE SCHWARTZ

Copyright © 1978, 1980 Sony/ATV Music Publishing LLC
All Rights Administered by Sony/ATV Music Publishing LLC, 8 Music Square West, Nashville, TN 37203
International Copyright Secured   All Rights Reserved

HOPELESSLY DEVOTED TO YOU
recorded by Olivia Newton-John
excerpt

Words and Music by
JOHN FARRAR

Copyright © 1978 by Unichappell-Stigwood Music, Ensign Music Corporation and John Farrar Music
All Rights Administered by Unichappell-Stigwood Music
International Copyright Secured   All Rights Reserved

HOW AM I SUPPOSED TO LIVE WITHOUT YOU

recorded by Michael Bolton

excerpt

Words and Music by MICHAEL BOLTON
and DOUG JAMES

© 1983 EMI APRIL MUSIC INC., IS HOT MUSIC and EMI BLACKWOOD MUSIC INC.
All Rights for IS HOT MUSIC Controlled and Administered by EMI APRIL MUSIC INC.
All Rights Reserved   International Copyright Secured   Used by Permission

I CAN'T MAKE YOU LOVE ME

recorded by Bonnie Raitt

excerpt

Words and Music by MIKE REID
and ALLEN SHAMBLIN

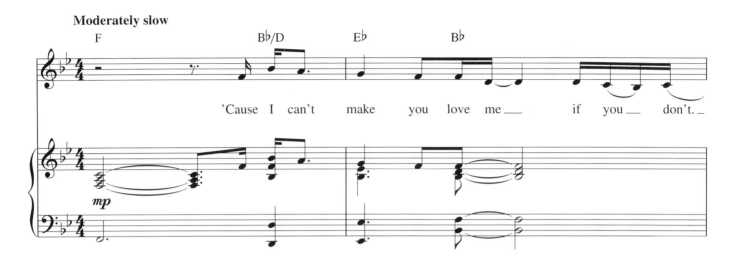

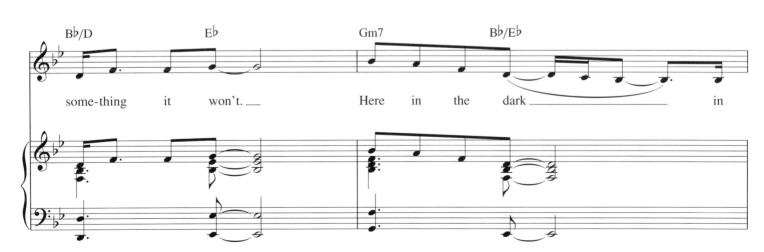

Copyright © 1991 ALMO MUSIC CORP., BRIO BLUES MUSIC and UNIVERSAL MUSIC - MGB SONGS
BRIO BLUES MUSIC Admin. by EVERGREEN COPYRIGHTS
All Rights Reserved   Used by Permission

I FEEL THE EARTH MOVE

recorded by Carole King

excerpt

Words and Music by
CAROLE KING

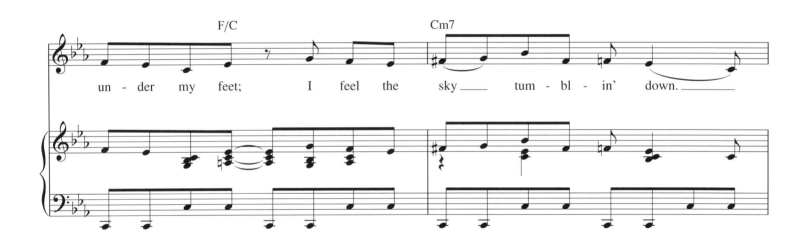

© 1971 (Renewed 1999) COLGEMS-EMI MUSIC INC.
All Rights Reserved   International Copyright Secured   Used by Permission

I NEED YOU
recorded by Marc Anthony
excerpt

Words and Music by
CORY ROONEY

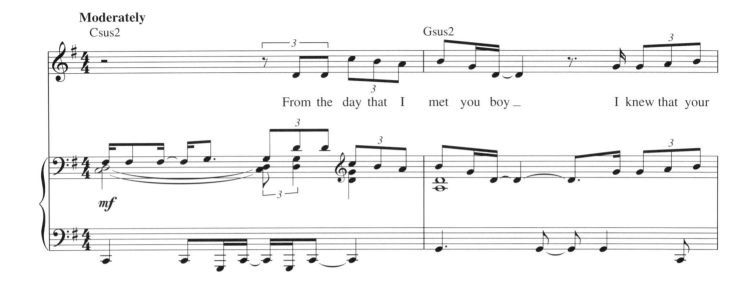

Copyright © 2002 Sony/ATV Music Publishing LLC and Cori Tiffani Publishing
All Rights Administered by Sony/ATV Music Publishing LLC, 8 Music Square West, Nashville, TN 37203
International Copyright Secured   All Rights Reserved

I SAY A LITTLE PRAYER

recorded by Dionne Warwick

excerpt

Lyric by HAL DAVID
Music by BURT BACHARACH

Copyright © 1966 (Renewed) Casa David and New Hidden Valley Music
International Copyright Secured   All Rights Reserved

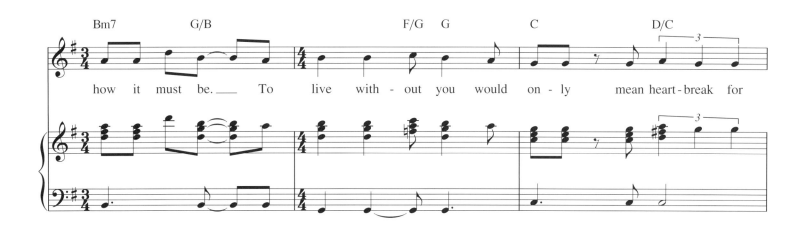
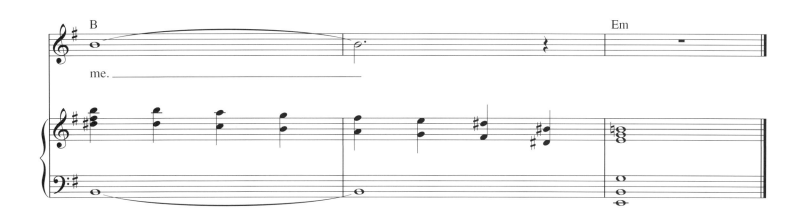

I WILL

recorded by The Beatles

excerpt

Words and Music by JOHN LENNON
and PAUL McCARTNEY

Gently

And when at last I find you, your song will fill the air. Sing it loud so I can hear you, make it eas-y to be near you, for the things you do en-dear you to me. Ah, you know I will. I will.

I WILL REMEMBER YOU
Theme from *The Brothers McMullen*
recorded by Sarah McLachlan
excerpt

Words and Music by SARAH McLACHLAN, SEAMUS EGAN and DAVE MERENDA

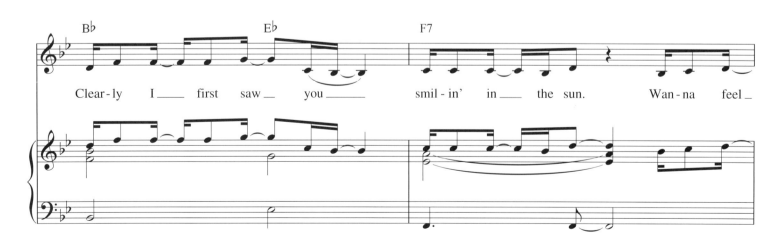

Copyright © 1995 Sony/ATV Music Publishing LLC, Tyde Music, Seamus Egan Music and T C F Music Publishing, Inc.
All Rights on behalf of Sony/ATV Music Publishing LLC and Tyde Music Administered by Sony/ATV Music Publishing LLC, 8 Music Square West, Nashville, TN 37203
All Rights on behalf of Seamus Egan Music Administered by Fox Film Music Corp.
International Copyright Secured   All Rights Reserved

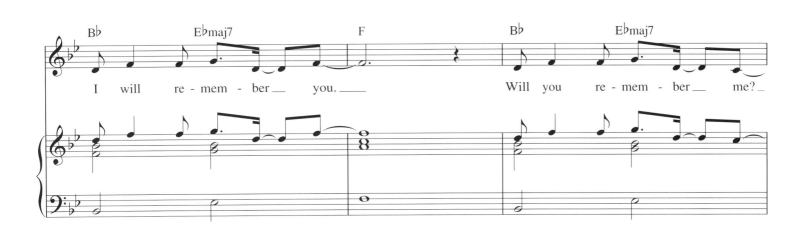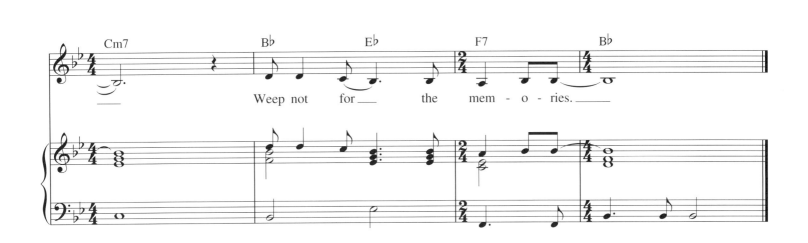

I'LL STAND BY YOU
recorded by Pretenders; Carrie Underwood
excerpt

Words and Music by CHRISSIE HYNDE,
TOM KELLY and BILLY STEINBERG

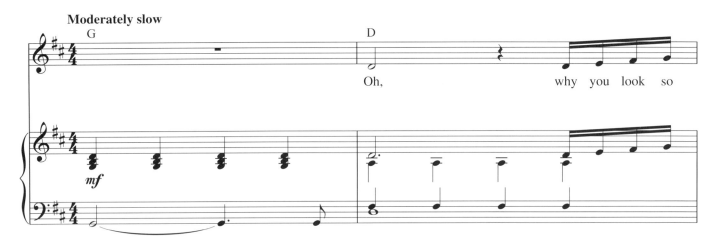

© 1994 EMI MUSIC PUBLISHING LTD. trading as CLIVE BANKS MUSIC LTD., TOM KELLY SONGS and JERK AWAKE
All Rights for EMI MUSIC PUBLISHING LTD. trading as CLIVE BANKS MUSIC LTD. Controlled and Administered by EMI APRIL MUSIC INC.
All Rights Reserved   International Copyright Secured   Used by Permission

IF I CAN'T HAVE YOU

recorded by Yvonne Elliman; Bee Gees

excerpt

Words and Music by BARRY GIBB,
ROBIN GIBB and MAURICE GIBB

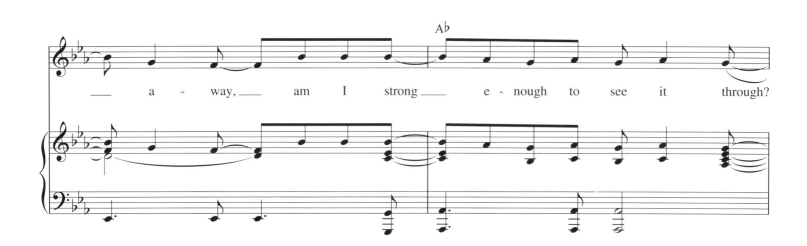

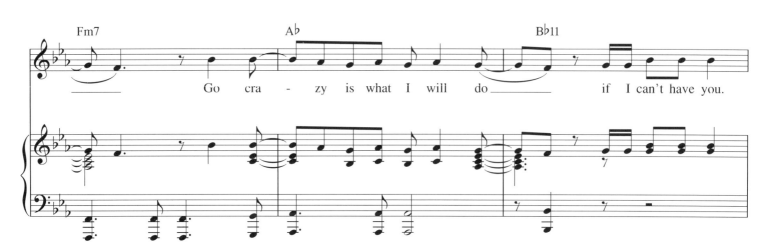

Copyright © 1977 by Universal Music Publishing International MGB Ltd., Warner-Tamerlane Publishing Corp. and Crompton Songs LLC
Copyright Renewed
All Rights for Universal Music Publishing International MGB Ltd. in the U.S. and Canada Administered by Universal Music - Careers
International Copyright Secured   All Rights Reserved

IT'S ALL WRONG, BUT IT'S ALL RIGHT

recorded by Dolly Parton

excerpt

Words and Music by
DOLLY PARTON

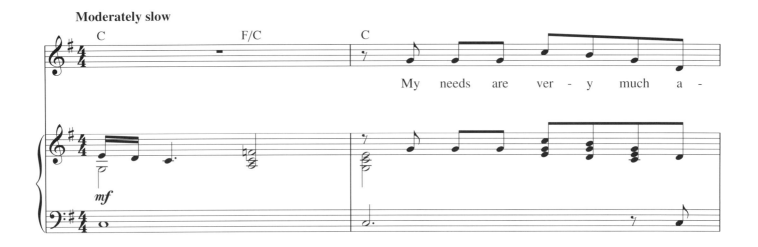

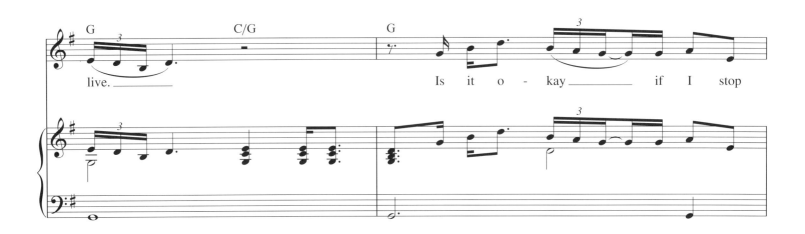

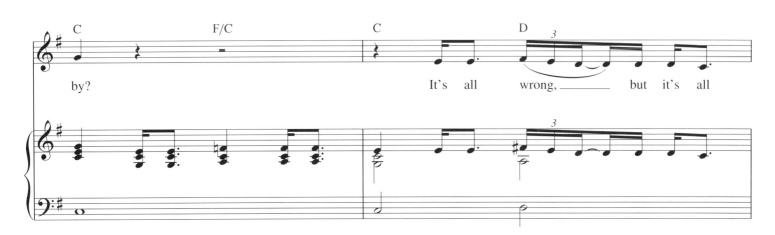

Copyright © 1977 (Renewed 2005) Velvet Apple Music
All Rights Reserved   Used by Permission

IT'S SO EASY

recorded by The Crickets; Linda Ronstadt

excerpt

Words and Music by BUDDY HOLLY
and NORMAN PETTY

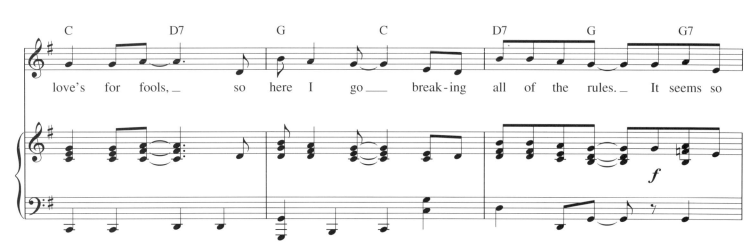

© 1958 (Renewed) MPL MUSIC PUBLISHING, INC. and WREN MUSIC CO.
All Rights Reserved

IT'S TOO LATE
recorded by Carole King
excerpt

Words and Music by CAROLE KING
and TONI STERN

Stayed in bed all morn-in' just to pass the time.

There's some-thin' wrong here, there can be no de-ny-in'.

One of us is chang-in', or may-be we've just stopped try-

© 1971 (Renewed 1999) COLGEMS-EMI MUSIC INC.
All Rights Reserved   International Copyright Secured   Used by Permission

LET IT BE
recorded by The Beatles
excerpt

Words and Music by JOHN LENNON
and PAUL McCARTNEY

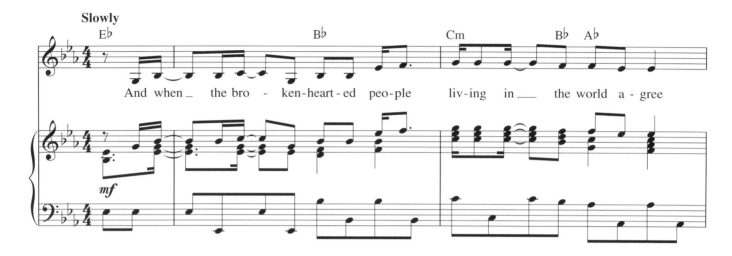

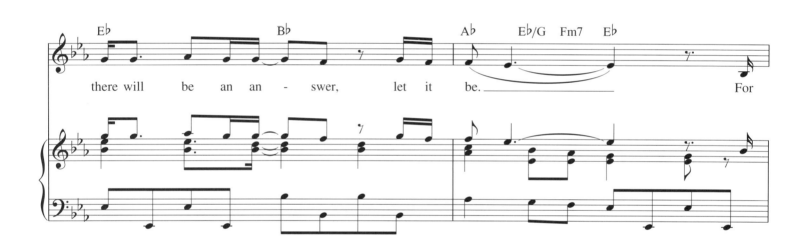

Copyright © 1970 Sony/ATV Music Publishing LLC
Copyright Renewed
All Rights Administered by Sony/ATV Music Publishing LLC, 8 Music Square West, Nashville, TN 37203
International Copyright Secured All Rights Reserved

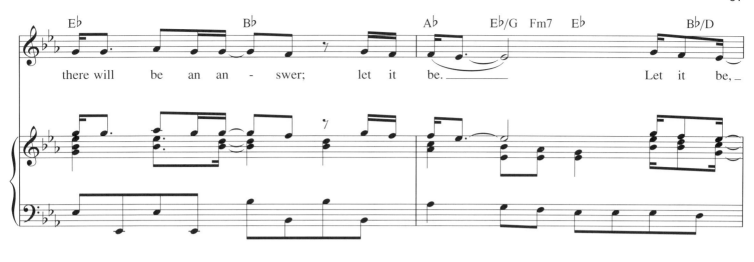
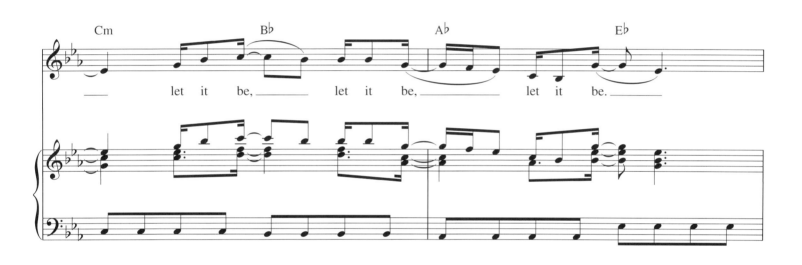

LISTEN
recorded by Beyoncé
excerpt

Music and Lyrics by HENRY KRIEGER, ANNE PREVEN,
SCOTT CUTLER and BEYONCÉ KNOWLES

Moderately slow

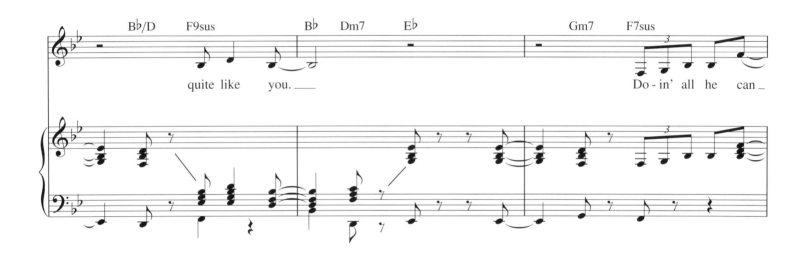

MY GUY
recorded by Mary Wells
excerpt

Words and Music by
WILLIAM "SMOKEY" ROBINSON

© 1964 (Renewed 1992) JOBETE MUSIC CO., INC.
All Rights Controlled and Administered by EMI APRIL MUSIC INC.
All Rights Reserved International Copyright Secured Used by Permission

MY FATHER
recorded by Judy Collins
excerpt

Words and Music by
JUDY COLLINS

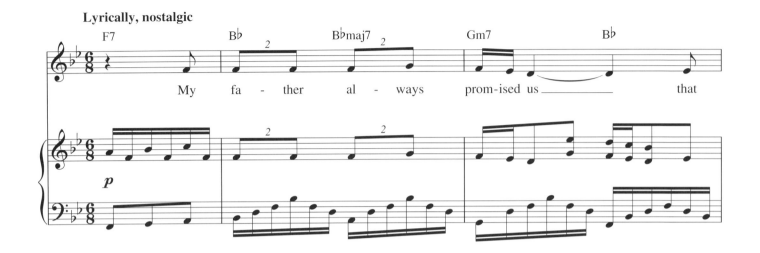

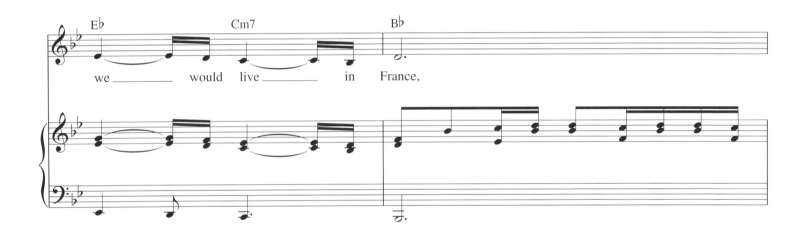

Copyright © 1968 UNIVERSAL MUSIC CORP. and ROCKY MOUNTAIN NATIONAL PARK MUSIC
Copyright Renewed
All Rights Controlled and Administered by UNIVERSAL MUSIC CORP.
All Rights Reserved   Used by Permission

(You Make Me Feel Like)
A NATURAL WOMAN
recorded by Aretha Franklin; Celine Dion; Kelly Clarkson
excerpt

Words and Music by GERRY GOFFIN, CAROLE KING and JERRY WEXLER

© 1967 (Renewed 1995) SCREEN GEMS-EMI MUSIC INC.
All Rights Reserved International Copyright Secured Used by Permission

PIECE OF MY HEART
recorded by Janis Joplin

excerpt

Words and Music by BERT BERNS
and JERRY RAGOVOY

But with all the love I give you, it's nev-er e-nough, but

I'm gon-na show you, ba-by, that a wom-an can be tough. So

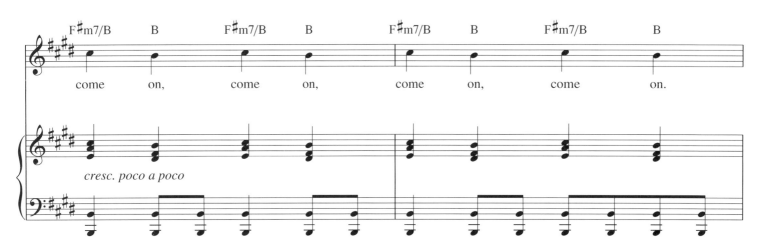

come on, come on, come on, come on, come on.

Copyright © 1967 Sony/ATV Music Publishing LLC, Unichappell Music Inc. and Sloopy II Music
Copyright Renewed
All Rights on behalf of Sony/ATV Music Publishing LLC Administered by Sony/ATV Music Publishing LLC, 8 Music Square West, Nashville, TN 37203
International Copyright Secured   All Rights Reserved

THE POWER OF LOVE

recorded by Celine Dion

excerpt

Words by MARY SUSAN APPLEGATE and JENNIFER RUSH
Music by CANDY DEROUGE and GUNTHER MENDE

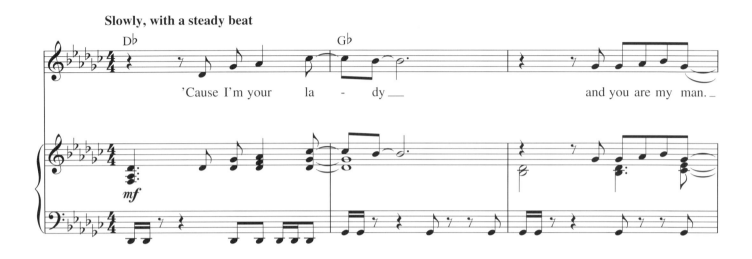

© 1986 EMI SONGS MUSIKVERLAG GMBH
All Rights for the U.S.A. and Canada Controlled and Administered by EMI APRIL MUSIC INC.
All Rights Reserved   International Copyright Secured   Used by Permission

REFLECTION
from Walt Disney Pictures' *Mulan*
recorded by Christina Aguilera

excerpt

Music by MATTHEW WILDER
Lyrics by DAVID ZIPPEL

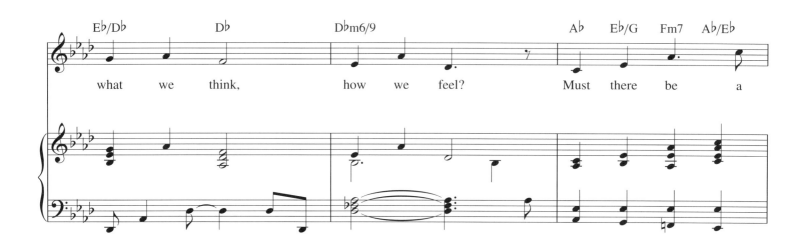

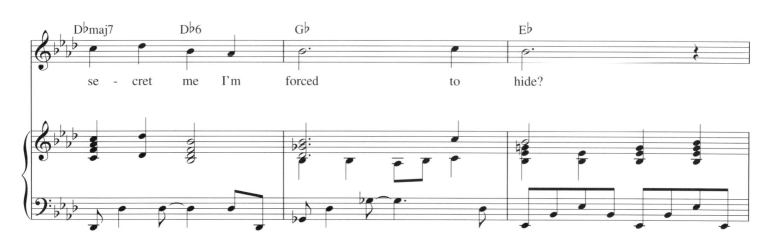

© 1998 Walt Disney Music Company
All Rights Reserved   Used by Permission

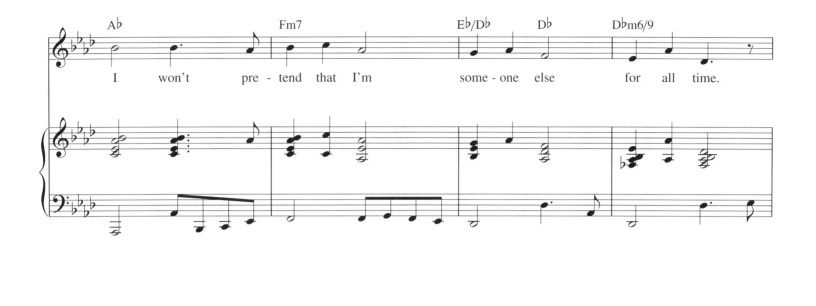
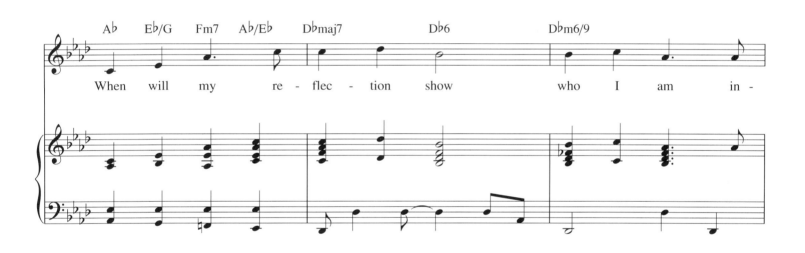
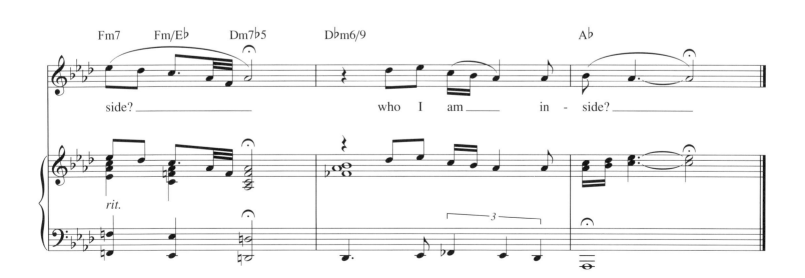

SAVE THE BEST FOR LAST

recorded by Vanessa Williams

excerpt

Words and Music by WENDY WALDMAN, PHIL GALDSTON and JON LIND

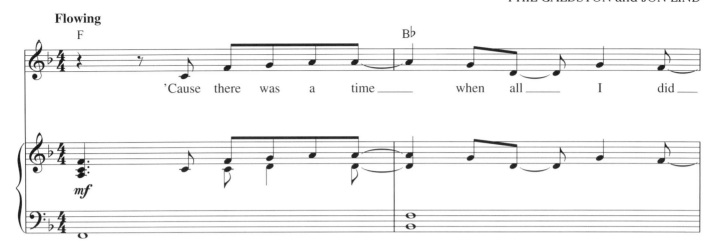

'Cause there was a time _____ when all _____ I did _____

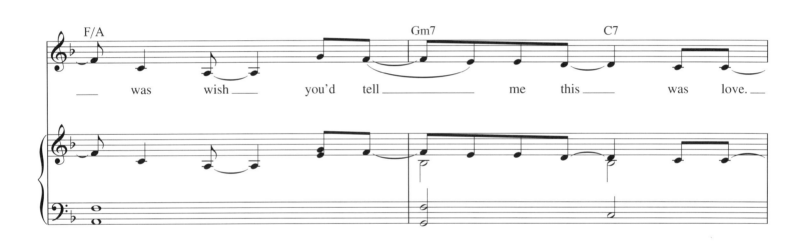

_____ was wish _____ you'd tell _____ me this _____ was love. _____

It's not the way _____ I hoped _____ or _____ how _____

© 1989 EMI LONGITUDE MUSIC, MOON AND STARS MUSIC, UNIVERSAL - POLYGRAM INTERNATIONAL PUBLISHING, INC.,
KAZZOOM MUSIC, INC. and BIG MYSTIQUE MUSIC
All Rights for MOON AND STARS MUSIC Controlled and Administered by EMI LONGITUDE MUSIC
All Rights for KAZZOOM MUSIC, INC. Controlled and Administered by UNIVERSAL - POLYGRAM INTERNATIONAL PUBLISHING, INC.
All Rights Reserved   International Copyright Secured   Used by Permission

SAVING ALL MY LOVE FOR YOU
recorded by Whitney Houston
excerpt

Words by GERRY GOFFIN
Music by MICHAEL MASSER

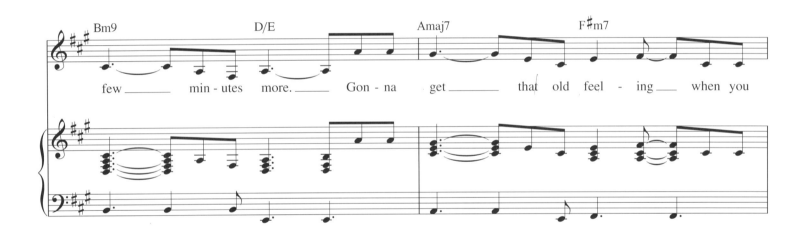

© 1978, 1985 SCREEN GEMS-EMI MUSIC INC., LAUREN-WESLEY MUSIC INC. and UNIVERSAL MUSIC CORP.
All Rights for LAUREN-WESLEY MUSIC INC. Controlled and Administered by SCREEN GEMS-EMI MUSIC INC.
All Rights Reserved   International Copyright Secured   Used by Permission

SO FAR AWAY
recorded by Carole King
excerpt

Words and Music by
CAROLE KING

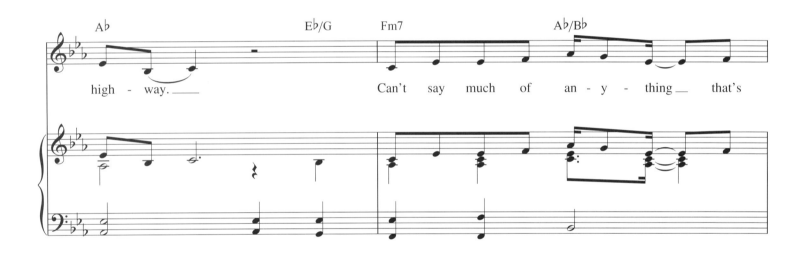

© 1971 (Renewed 1999) COLGEMS-EMI MUSIC INC.
All Rights Reserved   International Copyright Reserved   Used by Permission

SOLITAIRE

recorded by Elvis Presley, The Carpenters, Clay Aiken

excerpt

Words and Music by NEIL SEDAKA
and PHIL CODY

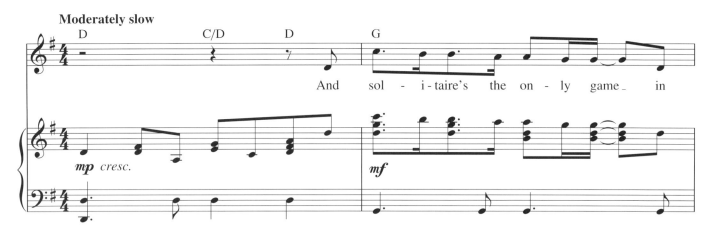

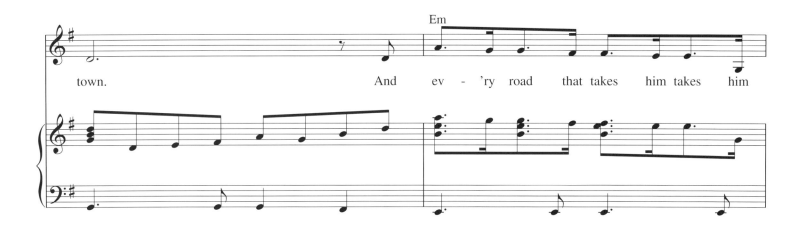

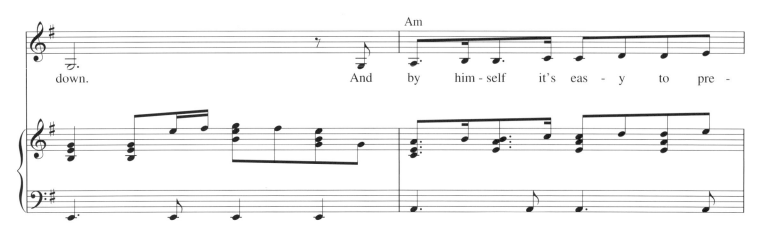

© 1972 (Renewed 2000) EMI Sosaha Music Inc., EMI Jemaxal Music Inc., Songs of SJL-RSL Music Co.,
SJL-RSL Songs Company and Sony/ATV Music Publishing LLC
All Rights on behalf of Sony/ATV Music Publishing LLC Administered by Sony/ATV Music Publishing LLC, 8 Music Square West, Nashville, TN 37203
All Rights Reserved   International Copyright Secured   Used by Permission

SOMEBODY TO LOVE

recorded by Jefferson Airplane
excerpt

Words and Music by
DARBY SLICK

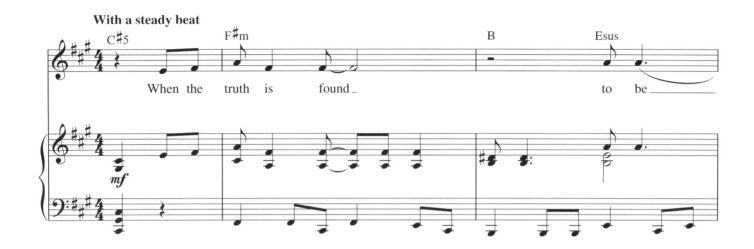
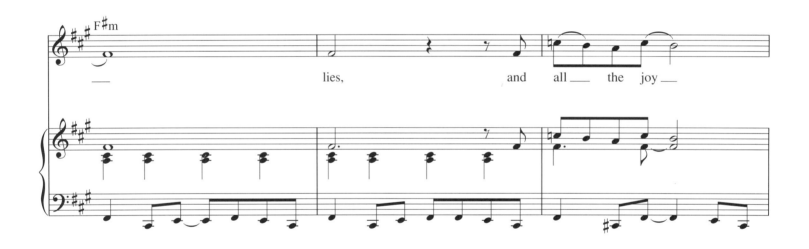

Copyright © 1967 IRVING MUSIC, INC.
Copyright Renewed
All Rights Reserved   Used by Permission

SOMETHING TO TALK ABOUT
(Let's Give Them Something To Talk About)
recorded by Bonnie Raitt
excerpt

Words and Music by
SHIRLEY EIKHARD

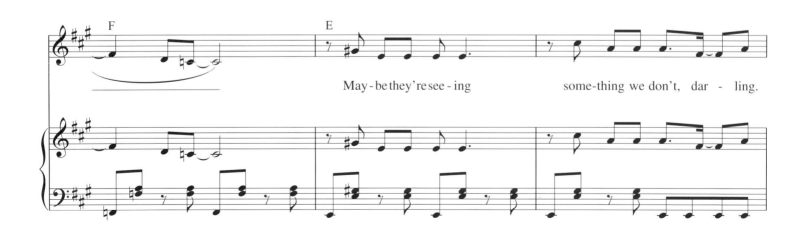

© 1985, 1988 EMI BLACKWOOD MUSIC INC. and CANVEE MUSIC
All Rights Reserved   International Copyright Secured   Used by Permission

SOMETIMES WHEN WE TOUCH
recorded by Dan Hill
excerpt

Words by DAN HILL
Music by BARRY MANN

And sometimes when we touch, the honesty's too much.

And I have to close my eyes and hide.

I wanna hold you till I die, till we both break down and cry.

I wanna hold you till the fear in me subsides.

Copyright © 1977 Sony/ATV Music Publishing LLC and Mann & Weil Songs, Inc.
Copyright Renewed
All Rights Administered by Sony/ATV Music Publishing LLC, 8 Music Square West, Nashville, TN 37203
International Copyright Secured   All Rights Reserved

SUPERSTAR
recorded by The Carpenters
excerpt

Words and Music by LEON RUSSELL
and BONNIE SHERIDAN

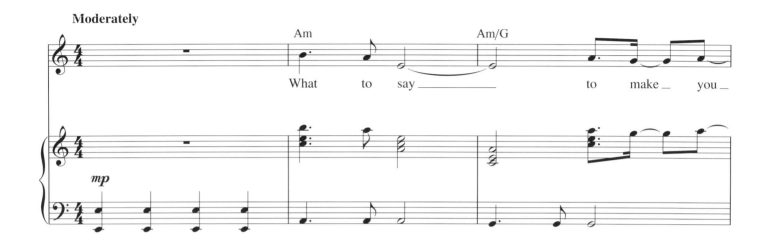

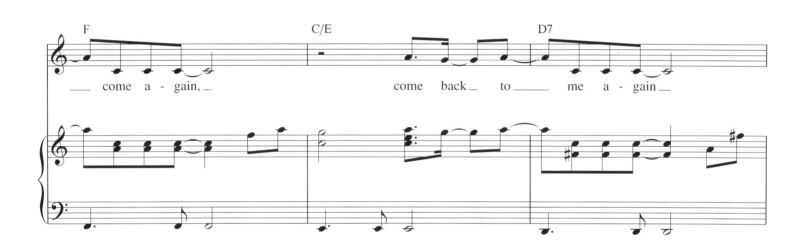

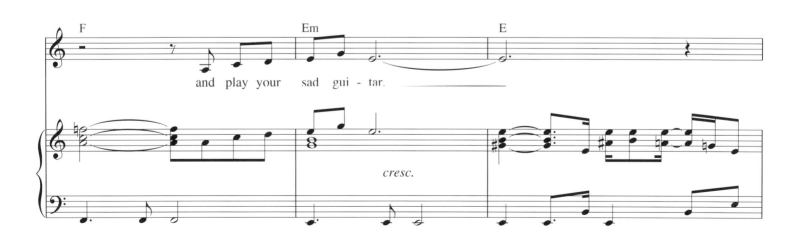

Copyright © 1970, 1971; Renewed 1998, 1999 FSMGI (IMRO), Embassy Music Corporation (BMI) and delbon Publishing Company, Inc. (BMI)
All Rights for FSMGI Controlled and Administered by State One Music America
International Copyright Secured   All Rights Reserved

SWEET DREAMS
(Are Made of This)
recorded by Eurythmics
excerpt

Words and Music by DAVID STEWART
and ANNIE LENNOX

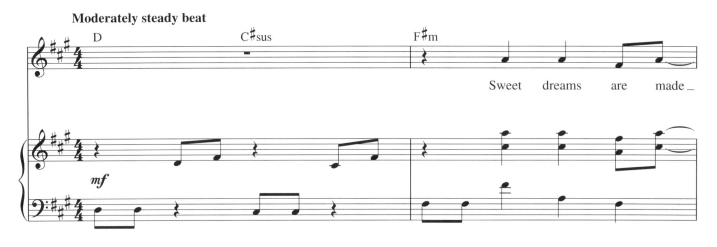

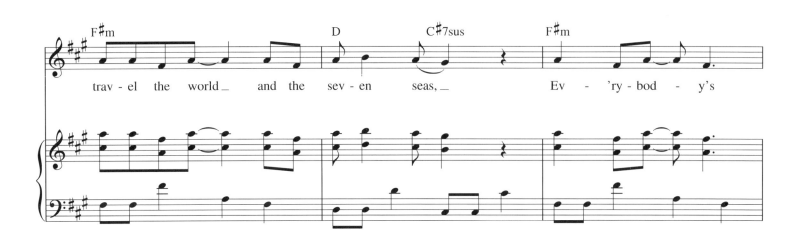

Copyright © 1983 by Universal Music Publishing MGB Ltd.
All Rights in the United States and Canada Administered by Universal Music - MGB Songs
International Copyright Secured   All Rights Reserved

THING CALLED LOVE
(Are You Ready for This Thing Called Love)
recorded by Bonnie Raitt

excerpt

Words and Music by
JOHN HIATT

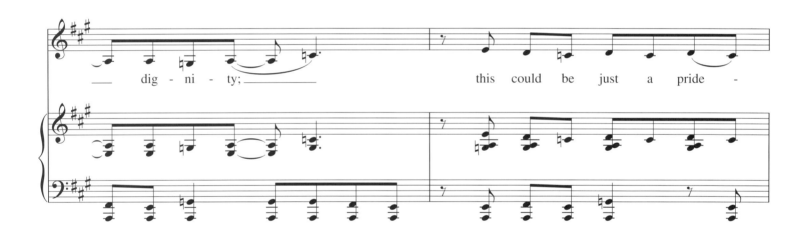

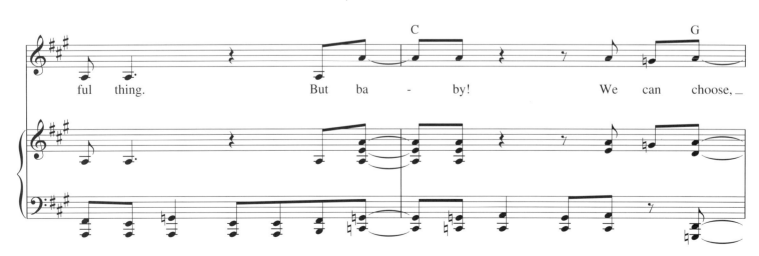

Copyright © 1987 by Universal Music - Careers
International Copyright Secured   All Rights Reserved

THIS AIN'T A LOVE SONG

recorded by Bon Jovi

excerpt

Words and Music by JON BON JOVI,
RICHIE SAMBORA and DESMOND CHILD

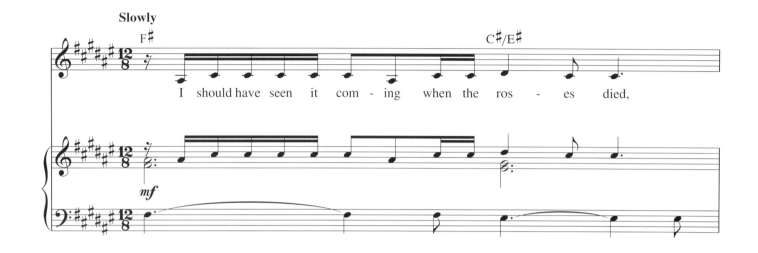

Copyright © 1995 UNIVERSAL - POLYGRAM INTERNATIONAL PUBLISHING, INC.,
BON JOVI PUBLISHING, AGGRESSIVE MUSIC, EMI APRIL MUSIC INC. and DESMOBILE MUSIC CO., INC.
All Rights for BON JOVI PUBLISHING and AGGRESSIVE MUSIC Controlled and Administered by UNIVERSAL - POLYGRAM INTERNATIONAL PUBLISHING, INC.
All Rights for DESMOBILE MUSIC CO., INC. Controlled and Administered by EMI APRIL MUSIC INC.
All Rights Reserved   Used by Permission

144

TIME AFTER TIME
recorded by Cyndi Lauper

excerpt

Words and Music by CYNDI LAUPER
and ROB HYMAN

Copyright © 1983 Rellla Music Co., WB Music Corp. and Dub Notes
All Rights for Rellla Music Co. Administered by Sony/ATV Music Publishing LLC, 8 Music Square West, Nashville, TN 37203
All Rights for Dub Notes Administered by WB Music Corp.
International Copyright Secured   All Rights Reserved

TRUE COLORS
recorded by Cyndi Lauper; Phil Collins
excerpt

Words and Music by BILLY STEINBERG
and TOM KELLY

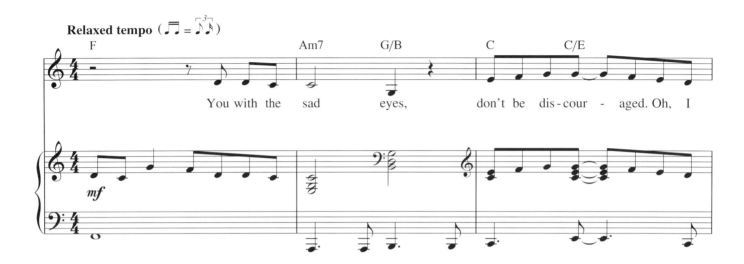

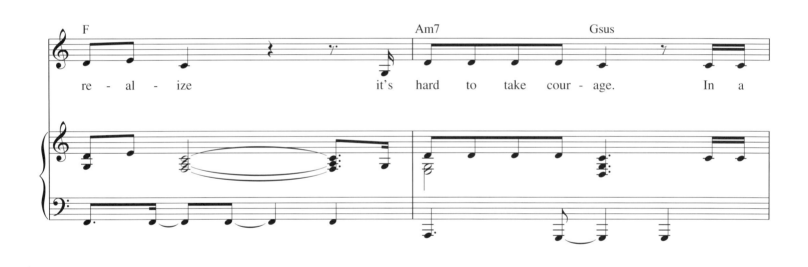

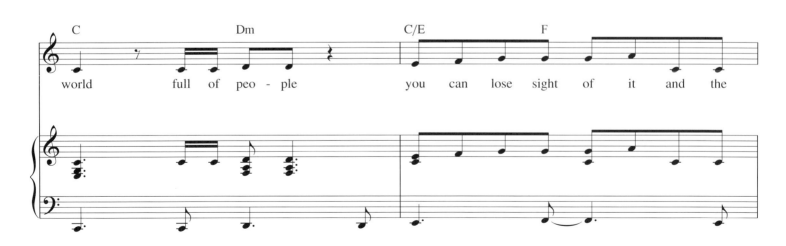

Copyright © 1986 Sony/ATV Music Publishing LLC
All Rights Administered by Sony/ATV Music Publishing LLC, 8 Music Square West, Nashville, TN 37203
International Copyright Secured   All Rights Reserved

WALK ON BY
recorded by Dionne Warwick
excerpt

Lyric by HAL DAVID
Music by BURT BACHARACH

Copyright © 1964 (Renewed) Casa David and New Hidden Valley Music
International Copyright Secured All Rights Reserved

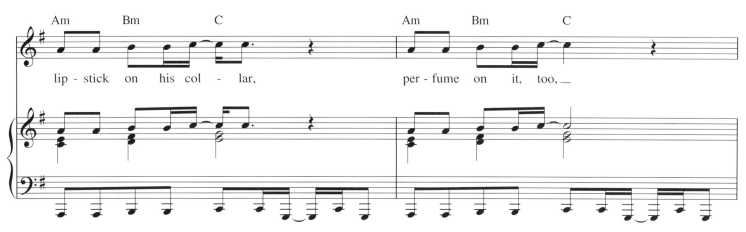

WE'VE ONLY JUST BEGUN

recorded by The Carpenters

excerpt

Words and Music by ROGER NICHOLS
and PAUL WILLIAMS

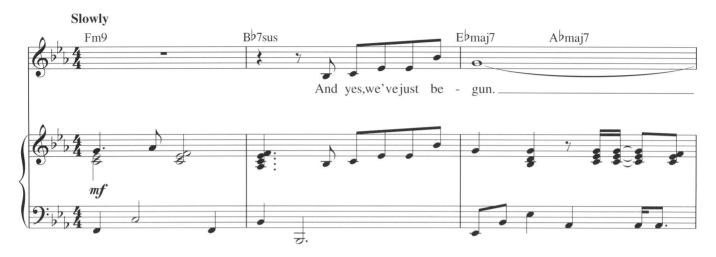

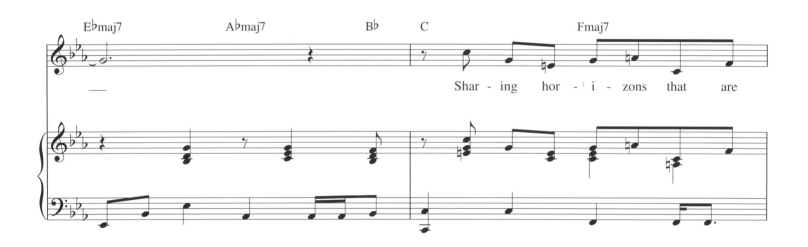

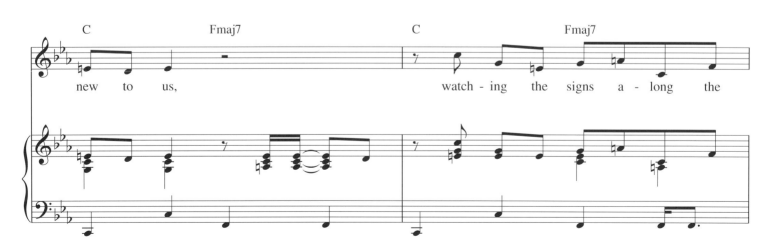

Copyright © 1970 IRVING MUSIC, INC.
Copyright Renewed
All Rights Reserved   Used by Permission

WHAT ABOUT LOVE?
recorded by Heart
excerpt

Words and Music by BRIAN ALLEN, SHERON ALTON and JIM VALLANCE

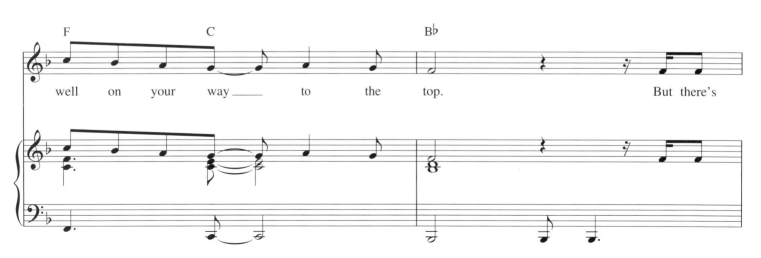

Copyright © 1985 Sony/ATV Music Publishing LLC, Sony/ATV Music Publishing Canada, Al-Toons Music Inc., Almo Music Corp. and Testatyme Music
All Rights on behalf of Sony/ATV Music Publishing LLC, Sony/ATV Music Publishing Canada and Al-Toons Music Inc. Administered by
Sony/ATV Music Publishing LLC, 8 Music Square West, Nashville, TN 37203
All Rights on behalf of Testatyme Music Administered by Almo Music Corp.
International Copyright Secured   All Rights Reserved

WHEN THERE WAS ME AND YOU
from the Disney Channel Original Movie *High School Musical*
recorded by Vanessa Anne Hudgens

excerpt

Words and Music by
JAMIE HOUSTON

© 2005 Walt Disney Music Company
All Rights Reserved Used by Permission

WILL YOU LOVE ME TOMORROW
(Will You Still Love Me Tomorrow)
recorded by The Shirelles

excerpt

Words and Music by GERRY GOFFIN
and CAROLE KING

© 1961 (Renewed 1989) SCREEN GEMS-EMI MUSIC INC.
All Rights Reserved   International Copyright Secured   Used by Permission

WITHOUT YOU
recorded by Badfinger; Mariah Carey

excerpt

Written by PETER HAM
and TOM EVANS

© 1970 (Renewed 1999) BUGHOUSE (ASCAP) o/b/o Bug Music LTD. (PRS)
All Rights Reserved   Used by Permission

WHERE THE BOYS ARE
recorded by Connie Francis

excerpt

Words and Music by HOWARD GREENFIELD
and NEIL SEDAKA

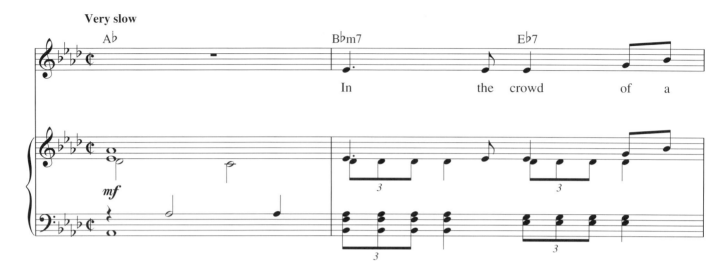

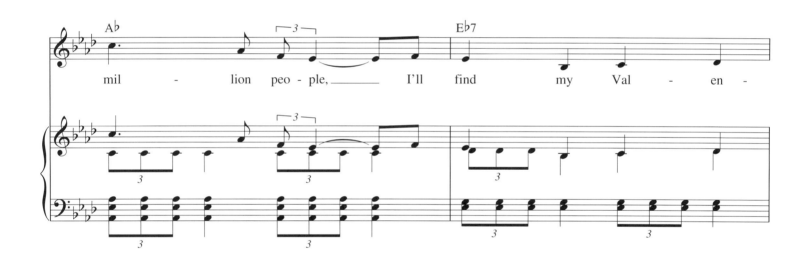

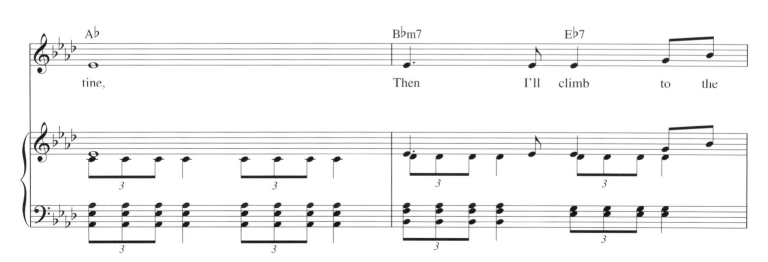

© 1960 (Renewed 1988) SCREEN GEMS-EMI MUSIC INC. and UNIVERSAL MUSIC - CAREERS
All Rights Reserved   International Copyright Secured   Used by Permission

WHY DO FOOLS FALL IN LOVE
recorded by Frankie Lymon & The Teenagers

excerpt

Words and Music by MORRIS LEVY
and FRANKIE LYMON

Love __ is a los-ing game, love __ can

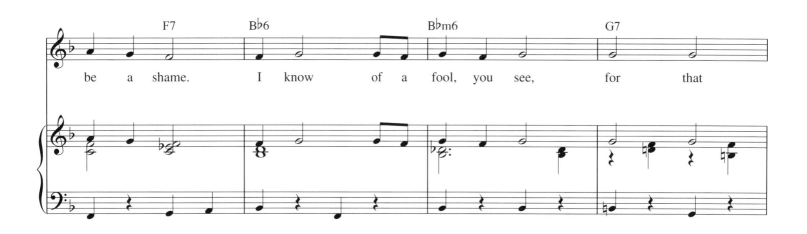

be a shame. I know of a fool, you see, for that

fool is me! Tell me why, __

© 1956 (Renewed 1984) EMI LONGITUDE MUSIC and EMI FULL KEEL MUSIC
All Rights Reserved International Copyright Secured Used by Permission

WOULDN'T IT BE NICE

recorded by The Beach Boys

excerpt

Words and Music by BRIAN WILSON,
TONY ASHER and MIKE LOVE

Copyright © 1966 IRVING MUSIC, INC.
Copyright Renewed
All Rights Reserved Used by Permission

YOU CAN'T HURRY LOVE

recorded by The Supremes; Phil Collins

excerpt

Words and Music by EDWARD HOLLAND, LAMONT DOZIER and BRIAN HOLLAND

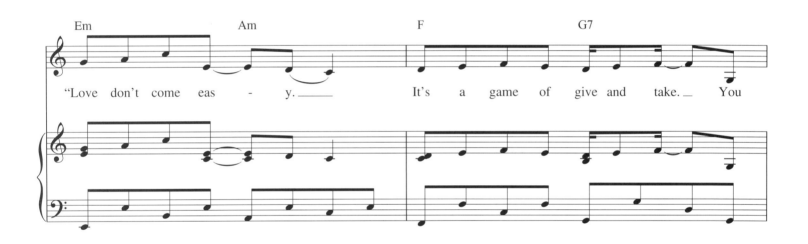

© 1965, 1966 (Renewed 1993, 1994) Jobete Music Co., Inc.
All Rights Controlled and Administered by EMI Blackwood Music Inc. on behalf of Stone Agate Music (A Division of Jobete Music Co., Inc.)
All Rights Reserved International Copyright Secured Used by Permission

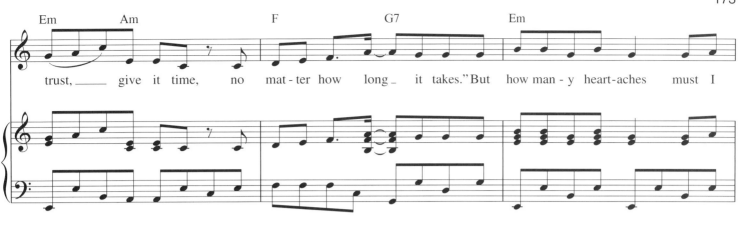

YOU KEEP ME HANGIN' ON
recorded by The Shirelles

excerpt

Words and Music by EDWARD HOLLAND, LAMONT DOZIER and BRIAN HOLLAND

Set me free why don't cha babe;

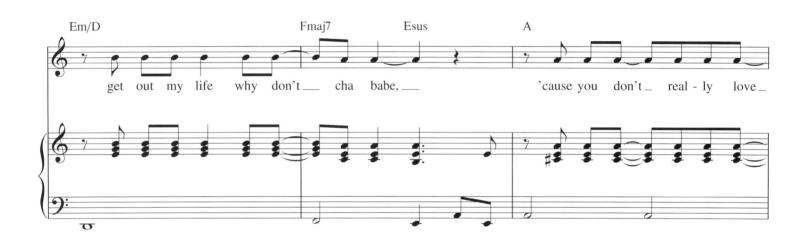

get out my life why don't cha babe, 'cause you don't real-ly love

me. You just keep me hang-in' on.

© 1966 (Renewed 1994) Jobete Music Co., Inc.
All Rights Controlled and Administered by EMI Blackwood Music Inc. on behalf of Stone Agate Music (A Division of Jobete Music Co., Inc.)
All Rights Reserved   International Copyright Secured   Used by Permission

YOU LEARN
recorded by Alanis Morissette
excerpt

Lyrics by ALANIS MORISSETTE
Music by ALANIS MORISSETTE
and GLEN BALLARD

Copyright © 1995 SONGS OF UNIVERSAL, INC., VANHURST PLACE, UNIVERSAL MUSIC CORP. and AEROSTATION CORPORATION
All Rights for VANHURST PLACE Controlled and Administered by SONGS OF UNIVERSAL, INC.
All Rights for AEROSTATION CORPORATION Controlled and Administered by UNIVERSAL MUSIC CORP.
All Rights Reserved   Used by Permission

YOU RAISE ME UP

recorded by Josh Groban

excerpt

Words and Music by BRENDAN GRAHAM
and ROLF LOVLAND

Slowly, steadily

When I am down and, oh, my soul's so

weary; when trou-bles come and my heart bur-dened

be; then I am still and wait here in the si-lence un-til You

Copyright © 2002 by Peermusic (UK) Ltd. and Universal Music Publishing, A Division of Universal Music AS
All Rights for Peermusic (UK) Ltd. in the United States Controlled and Administered by Peermusic III, Ltd.
All Rights for Universal Music Publishing, A Division of Universal Music AS in the United States and Canada Controlled and Administered by
Universal - PolyGram International Publishing, Inc.
International Copyright Secured   All Rights Reserved

YOU'LL BE IN MY HEART
(Pop Version)
from Walt Disney Pictures' *Tarzan*™
recorded by Phil Collins
excerpt

Words and Music by
PHIL COLLINS

© 1999 Edgar Rice Burroughs, Inc. and Walt Disney Music Company
All Rights Reserved Used by Permission